YOUR KNOWLEDGE HAS VALUE

Bibliographic information published by the German National Library:

The German National Library lists this publication in the National Bibliography;
detailed bibliographic data are available on the Internet at http://dnb.dnb.de .

Imprint:

Copyright © 2013 GRIN Verlag, Open Publishing GmbH
Print and binding: Books on Demand GmbH, Norderstedt Germany
ISBN: 978-3-668-10729-8

This book at GRIN:

http://www.grin.com/en/e-book/311700/english-listening-and-speaking-proficiency-
of-medical-learners-in-pakistan

Mahwish Mumtaz Niazi

English Listening And Speaking Proficiency Of Medical Learners In Pakistan

GRIN Publishing

GRIN - Your knowledge has value

Since its foundation in 1998, GRIN has specialized in publishing academic texts by students, college teachers and other academics as e-book and printed book. The website www.grin.com is an ideal platform for presenting term papers, final papers, scientific essays, dissertations and specialist books.

Investigating English Listening And Speaking Proficiency Of Medical Learners In Pakistan

Mahwish Mumtaz Niazi
National University of Modern Languages, H-9, Islamabad

Abstract

The present study was carried out to investigate the existing proficiency of medical learners in English listening and speaking skills. The purpose of the study is to recommend a course of English language in response to the linguistic inadequacy of the medical learners studying in the medical colleges of Pakistan. The perceptions of students of medicine, teachers of medicine, medical trainees and medical administrators were gathered. The data were analyzed quantitatively by means of Statistical Package for Social Sciences. The results indicate that existing proficiency of medical learners in English listening and speaking skills was not up to the mark. This situation calls for appropriate attention for the implementation of a course of English based on English speaking and listening contents in the medical colleges of Pakistan therefore, the standard of medical education can be elevated both at national and international levels.

Content

Introduction

The language of medicine in Pakistan is English. Curriculum has been exclusively devised in English. The examination is held in the English language. Other related activities like various classroom activities, listening to lectures, classroom presentations, interacting with teachers and dealing with the course contents of various medical subjects are also conducted in English.

There are several key factors, which make medical profession as an excellent career choice in Pakistan. For example, there are ever-increasing life expectancies and improved focus on the health related issues. Due to poor health issues, people need to consult medical practitioners anytime and visit them in the hospitals and clinics. For this reason, doctors and the associated staff are considered very important people. However, better-learned doctors have better incomes. The students who pursue medical education are desirous of helping others live happier and healthier lives. Medical is considered a secure profession because of the huge availability of the jobs in this sector. According to a report ("Bloomberg Business Week", 2006), over 1.7 million new jobs have been included in the health care center since 2001 while jobs beyond the field of health care are same as five years. Moreover, the skills attained at the end of the degree, provide the students opportunities to practice privately by opening a clinic in any area if there are no formal job positions vacant in the hospitals available. This field is becoming more and more specified with the huge influx of research-oriented approaches that makes it highly competitive both nationally and internationally. The medical graduates also hold key positions in the other departments of the government. They take part in the political activities of the country and become renowned politicians in the national and provincial assemblies. Dr. Fehmida Mirza is one such personality who despite having secured her degree in MBBS went for politics and had been elected as the speaker of the National Assembly of Pakistan in the elections of February 2008 and is serving to date ("Details of Dr. Fehmida Mirza",

1999-2012). Doctors appear in the competitive examination for central superior services and serve at the administrative posts other than medical. Similarly, they join non-government organizations for the causes of social welfare. Recently, a trend has been seen that doctors play an important role in the electronic media to bring awareness related to the general public health issues. They work as anchorpersons as well as are invited in television shows as guests to provide guidelines on the subjects related to various diseases and illnesses. Thus, a medical graduate in Pakistan has various distinct career opportunities.

Statement Of The Problem

There have been no significant endeavors undertaken in regard to the investigation of the English language listening and speaking needs of the medical learners in Pakistan. As the medium of instruction in Pakistani medical colleges is English yet medical learners generally do not feel confident when they have to speak in English. This inability lowers their self-confidence while presenting both at national and international levels. English as lingua franca of medicine demands expert trainings of Pakistani medical learners in spoken English to deal with the academic and occupational challenges of modern age. There is a serious need to devise a needs based course of spoken English for the medical learners of Pakistan. In this course listening skills should be equally emphasized due to the integrative role of listening and speaking skills. Medical learners in Pakistan are not taught courses of English in medical colleges hence no trained teaching faculty is available. The situation becomes even much worse when the medical students face difficulties in listening and speaking English as medical professionals after their graduation or when they have to go for higher education abroad or present in seminars, workshops, discussions and lectures. Thus it is important to explore the existing proficiency of medical learners in English listening and speaking skills therefore, a course of English based on the communicative needs of medical learners can be recommended for the medical students in the medical colleges of Pakistan.

Present Study

The present study aims at investigation of the existing proficiency of medical learners of Pakistan in English listening and speaking skills. The perceptions of four different stakeholders (i.e., students of medicine, teachers of medicine, medical trainees and medical administrators) have been gathered. It would lead to the recommendation of spoken English language course in the medical colleges of Pakistan.

Literature Review

ESP and ELT have differed in terms of their instructional objectives. ELT courses deal with English listening, speaking, reading, writing skills equally, and thus with different topics. In these courses the teachers determine objectives as it is not known how, why, when learners need the language in future whereas, ESP courses are devised after the needs analysis is conducted thus instructional objectives are determined (Harmer, 2001, p. 10). There is a controversy over the matter as to what exactly distinguishes ESP programs from English for General Purposes (EGP) courses (Hutchinson & Waters, 1987, p. 54). One clear distinction between ESP and EGP was that ESP courses were meant to serve a clearly "utilitarian purpose" (Robinson 1980, p. 6) whereas, EGP aimed at establishing a "general level of proficiency" (Crystal, 1996, p. 108). The ESP theory is based on the idea that individual learners have their respective language problems hence it is necessary that their problem areas should be targeted and thus categorized accordingly for the design of English course (Belcher, 2006, p. 135).

English has been the most widespread lingua franca of the western world used in sciences, and among them is medicine. Different sciences have used English to various degrees. English is considered to be the only language of wider communication within medicine and mathematics (Ammon, 1994; Medgyes & Kaplan, 1992). The international role and status of English in the fields of science and technology are indubitable. This point can be authenticated by the fact that English is the only source employed for large scale publications around the globe for self-recognition (Ammon & Hellinger, 1992, p. viii). According to Swales, English has established its unparalleled place at globally acknowledged literary and scientific platforms hence it appears that all other languages have been swept away by influential role of English (Swales, 1997, p. 374). Non-English speaking physicians, researchers and practicing doctors have no other option but to learn English if they want to be informed of the latest developments in their fields (Alcaraz & Navarro, 2006).

English is the international language used in both written and oral communication between health professionals involved in research, and it is the language used even at national meetings (Gunnarsson, 2001). In several non-English speaking countries, publishing in the native tongue has become a handicap to physicians with academic ambitions (Bakewell, 1992). On-going discussion shows criticism towards the increasing use of English. It is thought that domain loss is dividing people into two groups; the highly educated and the less educated (Taavitsainen & Pahta, 2003). It is clear that the well-educated group has known English well, since English is used in academic studies. When aspiring doctors and nurses join the medical discourse community they have to be familiar with these principles. Most novice members enter the community when they start their career at medical institutions such as hospitals. Once they join the discourse community of medical personnel (e.g., when commencing internships in hospitals), they have to become familiar with the mechanisms of communication, be they mechanisms of intercommunication or mechanisms for providing information and feedback. In the case of medical personnel the use of mechanisms such as conferences, staff meetings, reports, e-mails, and other forms of correspondence are involved in order to communicate and thus to exchange information. In medical discourse there are different types of communication, depending on who is communicating with whom. One type is inter-physician communication; doctors communicate with each other at conferences or via written journal articles (Krios- Linder, 2007). Doctors communicate with nurses and other personnel and vice versa. This communication plays only a minor role in the eyes of some researchers, as it seems to be restricted to situations such as changing shifts or talking about patient facts and figures. Communication with other hospital personnel (e.g., secretaries) tends to be ignored. Pathologists, for example, record autopsy reports; secretaries then type these up (Hoejke, 2007, p. 8). Another type of communication occurs between medical personnel and patients. Whereas several studies have focused on doctor-patient communication, comparatively little research has been done on the topic of nurse-patient communication. Patients are often intimidated and do not ask questions in the course of a doctor-patient consultation. They sometimes turn to nurses to ask for clarification, or for emotional support. In the literature, however, doctor-patient communication has been the predominant topic of research, as opposed to nurse- patient communication (Krois-Lindner, 2007).

EMP courses – like all kinds of ESP should be tailor-made to the learners' purposes and needs, that is by first thinking about who these medical learners can be and what their purposes are. Maher (1986a) pointed out the need for a specific syllabus that will enhance the communicative effectiveness of an English language course. For example, attempts to develop courses using instructional methodologies such as content-based learning and problem-based learning have been made. The use of technological equipment has been regarded as an important aspect in EMP courses to bring real life communication into the classroom. Various projects have also been undertaken to explore different ways of teaching medical terminology.

Structural and traditional methods such as teaching term formation of medical terminology as a vocabulary teaching strategy and grammar translation have also been found in the literature.

Needs analysis has its rudimental role in ESP theory as it lays foundation for design of specific language course (Dudley-Evans & St. John, 1998, p. 122). Every language course should follow it (Hutchinson & Waters, 1987, p. 53). Needs analysis is usually conducted by means of questionnaires, interviews, and linguistic analyses. In this process, role of professional expertise and assessment is essential (Brown, 2001, p. 15). In present situation analysis (PSA), the existing situation of English language ability of learners is analyzed therefore course contents should be devised accurately with no inclusion of irrelevant literatures (Dudley-Evans & St. John, 1998, pp. 124-125). The existing adequacy level of the communicative skills of the learners along with a detailed diagnosis of plus and weak areas is general concern of the PSA (Robinson, 1991, p. 8). Thus, "To alter what is, we first need to know what it is" (Shiundu & Omulando, 1992).

Methodology

This research was based on the purpose to investigate existing proficiency of medical learners in English listening and speaking skills. The research questions were:

1. What is the existing proficiency of medical learners in English listening skills?

2. What is the existing proficiency of medical learners in English speaking skills?

The research was carried out in Rawalpindi city in the province of Punjab. Two medical colleges (i.e., Rawalpindi Medical College from the public sector and Islamic International Medical College from the private sector and their associated teaching hospitals) were selected. The sample population consisted of students of medicine, teachers of medicine, medical trainees and medical administrators. The students were taken from 1st professional, 2nd professional, 3rd professional and the 4th professional of MBBS. The rationale behind including sample from all four professionals was to explore English language learning needs and expectations of the students of all levels with respect to their present situations. The teachers of medicine were teaching in the medical colleges and thus practicing in their affiliated teaching hospitals. Teachers of both colleges were full time faculty members. The recent medical graduates included house officers and postgraduate trainees. The medical administrators included medical superintendents, deputy medical superintendents, assistant medical superintendents, and the administration registrars.

The study was carried out by means of questionnaires. Four questionnaires were designed. Questionnaire 1 gathered information from recent medical students. Questionnaire 2 gathered information from recent medical graduates. Questionnaire 3 gathered information from teachers of medicine. Questionnaire 4 gathered information from medical administrators. The data collected through questionnaires was analyzed quantitatively. For quantitative analysis, Statistical Package for Social Sciences was used. The detailed results were presented with the help of tables, charts and graphs by using Microsoft Excel sheet.

Data Analysis

The students of medicine, medical trainees and medical administrators were asked to provide information about their existing proficiency in English listening and speaking skills as:

How do you describe your existing level of proficiency in the following English language skills? Please check (✔) one box for each skill given below.

	Skill	Excellent	Good	Fair	Poor	No opinion
1	Listening skill					
2	Speaking skill					

The teachers of medicine were asked to provide information about the existing proficiency of medical students in English listening and speaking skills as:

How do you describe the existing level of proficiency of medical students in the following English language skills? Please check (   ) one box for each skill.

	Skill	Excellent	Good	Fair	Poor	No opinion
1	Listening skill					
2	Speaking skill					

Listening Skill

Table - 1
Frequencies and Percentages of Combined Groups' Perceptions
Regarding Existing Proficiency Level in English Listening Skill

Respondents	Excellent		Good		Fair		Poor		No opinion		Total
	F	P	F	P	F	P	F	P	F	P	N
Students	57	28.1	34	16.7	85	41.9	27	13.3	-	-	203
Teachers	06	6.3	33	34.7	32	33.7	23	24.2	01	1.1	95
Trainees	12	11.9	28	27.7	30	29.7	29	28.7	02	2.0	101
Administrators	06	19.4	06	19.4	17	54.8	02	6.5	-	-	31
N	81	+	101	+	164	+	81	+	03	=	430

Note. N= Total Number of Respondents   F= Frequency   P= Percentage

182(42.3%) respondents reported that medical learners had adequate English listening skill whereas, 245(56.9%) respondents reported that medical learners had inadequate English listening skill. See Table 1 and Figure 1.

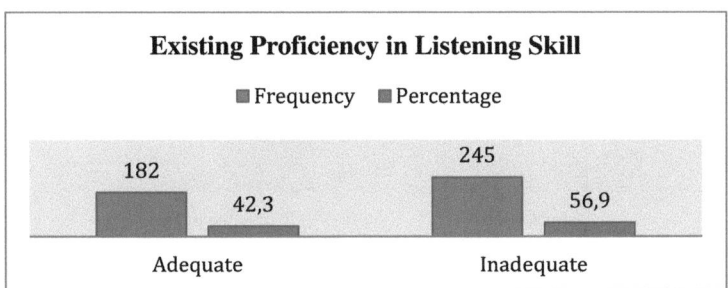

Figure 1

Overall perceptions regarding existing adequacy in English listening skill.

Speaking Skill

Table - 2

Frequencies and Percentages of Combined Groups' Perceptions Regarding Existing Proficiency Level in English Speaking Skill

Respondents	Excellent		Good		Fair		Poor		No opinion		Total
	F	P	F	P	F	P	F	P	F	P	N
Students	13	6.4	68	33.5	81	39.9	40	19.7	01	0.5	203
Teachers	08	8.4	30	31.6	34	35.8	22	23.2	01	1.1	95
Trainees	08	7.9	18	17.8	42	41.6	33	32.7	-	-	101
Administrators	04	12.9	08	25.8	12	38.7	07	22.6	-	-	31
N	33	+	124	+	169	+	102	+	02	=	430

Note. N= Total Number of Respondents   F= Frequency   P= Percentage

157(36.5%) respondents reported that medical learners had adequate English speaking skill whereas, 271(63.02%) respondents reported that medical learners had inadequate English speaking skill. See Table 2 and Figure 2.

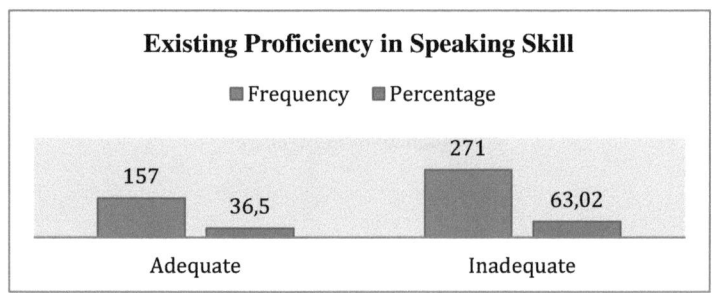

Figure 2

Overall perceptions regarding existing adequacy in English speaking skill.

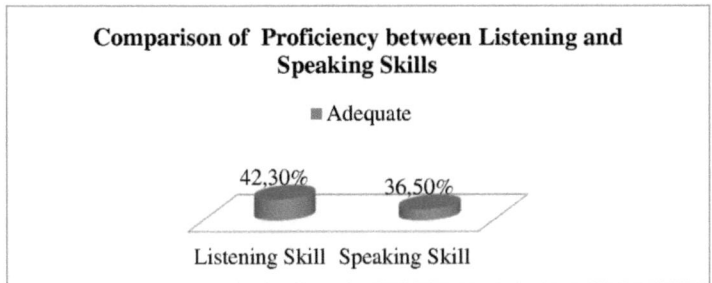

Figure 3

Overall perceptions regarding comparison of proficiency between English listening and speaking skills on the scale of adequacy.

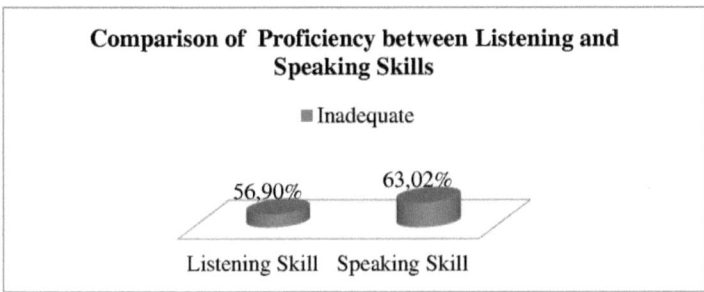

Figure 4

Overall perceptions regarding comparison of proficiency between English listening and speaking skills on the scale of inadequacy.

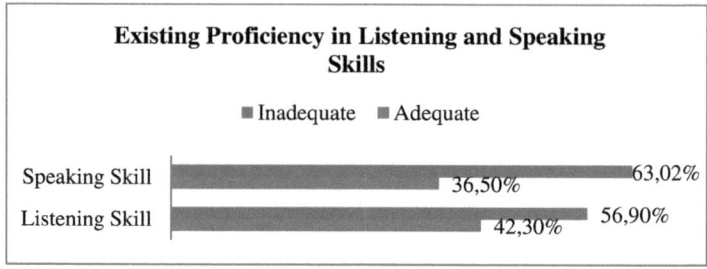

Figure 5

Overall perceptions regarding comparison of proficiency between English listening and speaking skills on the scales of adequacy and inadequacy.

The majority of medical learners perceived that English speaking skill was the first most required skill, English listening skill was second most required skill. See Figures 3, 4 and 5.

Discussion

The overall findings indicate that the existing proficiency of medical learners in English listening and speaking skills is not up to the mark. It is important that a course of English should be taught to them to improve their proficiency level in English at medical college. The course should emphasize listening and speaking skills of medical learners. In Pakistani context, students are generally not much interested in speaking English despite the fact English is their medium of instruction throughout the course of study in a medical college. However, when the medical graduates enter their professional lives, they need to speak English at several platforms especially in formal situations. Before joining medical college, the medical students are generally taught general English as a subject not as a language. It becomes hard for the medical learners to speak in actual communication situations because general English courses prior to admission in medical college do not meet the specific needs of medical learners with regard to their academic and occupational settings in medical field. Correct accent of speaking and pronunciation techniques should be included to improve phonological deficiencies of medical learners. It would lavishly aid them to present in seminars, conferences and workshops. In addition, it would make it easier for others to understand names of medicines and diseases. It should be declared mandatory for medical learners to communicate in English within the medical discourse community. Spoken English courses should be launched in the medical colleges. Trained English language instructors should be recruited for this purpose. The learner's autonomy should be respected. The learners should be encouraged to speak in English regardless of how frequently they make mistakes and speak erroneous language. Similarly, the medical teachers, medical trainees and medical administrators should be trained in English speaking and listening skills. The English language refresher courses and workshops may be conducted at hospital level. These courses may also be introduced as pre –sessional/ preparatory courses prior to have medical students actually involved in their medical studies. Since the results show a marginal difference between receptive and productive skill in terms of English language needs of medical learners, the course contents should address both listening and speaking skills due to their integrative roles. Frequent practice in speaking skills during various academic and occupational activities would necessarily help medical learners to deal with their future careers. An intense need for incorporating contents of speaking and listening skills in English language curriculum calls for appropriate attention. Further research can be conducted in order to devise spoken English language course contents at countrywide level.

References

Alcaraz, A. M. Á., & Navarro, F. (2006). Medicine: Use of English. In K. Brown (Ed.), *Encyclopedia of language and linguistics*. (2nd ed., pp. 752-759). Amsterdam: Elsevier.

Ammon, U. (1994). The present dominance of English in Europe: With an outlook on possible solutions to the European language problems. *Sociolinguistica, 8,* 1– 14.

Ammon, U., Hellinger, M. (Eds.). (1992). *Status change of languages*. Berlin: Walter de Gruyter.

Bakewell, D. (1992). Publish in English, or perish? *Nature* (pp. 356- 648).

Belcher, D. (2006). English for specific purposes: Teaching to perceived needs and imagined futures on worlds of work, study and everyday life. *TESOL Quarterly, 40*(1), 133-156.

Brown, J. D. (2001). *Using surveys in language programs*. Cambridge: Cambridge University Press.

Crystal, D. (1996). *The Cambridge encyclopedia of English language*. Cambridge, Great Britain: CUP.

Details of Dr. Fehmida Mirza. (1999-2012). Retrieved November 23, 2012, from

http://pakistanherald.com/Profile/Dr.-Fehmida-Mirza-203

Dudley-Evans, T., & St. John, M. J. (1998). *Development in English for specific purposes: A multi-disciplinary approach*. Cambridge: Cambridge University Press.

Gunnarsson, B. -L. (2001). Swedish tomorrow – A product of the linguistic dominance of English? In S. Boyd, & L. Huss (Eds.), *Managing multilingualism in a European nation-state. Challenges for Swedish. Current Issues in Language and Society, 7*(1), 51–69. Clevedon: Multilingual Matters Ltd.

Harmer, J. (2001). *The practice of English language teaching* (3rd ed.). Edinburgh: Pearson Education Ltd.

Hoekje, B. (2007). Medical discourse and ESP courses for international medical graduates (IMGs). *English for Specific Purposes, 26*(3), 17. Retrieved from http://www.sciencedirect.com/science/journal/08894906

Hutchinson, T., & Waters, A. (1987). *English for specific purposes: A learning-centered approach.* Cambridge: Cambridge University Press.

Krois-L., A. (2007). *World of work 2: A look at legal, technical and medical English.* University of Vienna, English Department.

Maher, J. (1986a). English for medical purposes. *Language Teaching, 19,* 112-145.

Medgyes, P., & Kaplan, R. (1992). Discourse in a foreign language: The example of Hungarian scholars. *International Journal of the Sociology of Language, 98,* 67–100.

Niazi, M., M. (2012). *English for medical purposes: a case of English for specific purposes* (Doctoral thesis).National University of Modern Languages, Islamabad, Pakistan.

Robinson, P. (1980). *ESP (English for Specific Purposes).* Oxford Pergamon Press.

Robinson, P. (1991). *ESP today: A practitioner's guide* (pp. 1-21). New York: Prentice Hall.

Shiundu J. S., & Omulando S. J. (1992*). Curriculum: Theory and practice in Kenya.* Nairobi:Oxford University Press.

Swales, J. (1997). English as tyrannosaurus rex. *World Englishes, 16,* 373–382.

Taavitsainen, I., & Pahta, P. (2003). English in Finland, globalization, language awareness and questions of identity. *English Today, 4,* 3–15.

What's Really Propping Up the Economy. (2006, September 24). *Bloomberg business week magazine.* Retrieved June 30, 2011, from http://www.businessweek.com/stories/2006-09-24/whats-really-propping-up-the-economy